Images of Wisdom

Images of Wisdom
SEEING GOD in EVERYTHING

Swami Kriyananda

CRYSTAL CLARITY PUBLISHERS Nevada City, California

©2009 by Hansa Trust
2025 release with new cover and format
All rights reserved. Published 2025

CRYSTAL CLARITY PUBLISHERS
crystalclarity.com | clarity@crystalclarity.com
14618 Tyler Foote Rd. | Nevada City, California
800.424.1055

ISBN 978-1-56589-251-4 (print) | *available* (print)
ISBN 978-1-56589-518-8 (e-book) | *available* (e-book)

Photos by Swami Kriyananda
Cover design by Tejindra Scott Tully
Interior layout and design by Michele Madhavi Molloy

The *Joy Is Within You* symbol is registered by Ananda Church of Self-Realization of Nevada County, California.

Foreword

Spiritual teachings, as we all know, can easily become abstract and even boringly distant from reality. Vivid imagery clarifies what is obscure, and makes acceptable thoughts that otherwise might be received with doubt. A good metaphor creates a bridge to higher understanding. It can also be fun to read.

Great teachers of humanity, including Jesus Christ, have often spoken in parables and metaphors, thereby making their teachings come tangibly alive. Swami Kriyananda, a foremost disciple of the great master Paramhansa Yogananda, has followed in that tradition. His discourses, whether in speech or in writing, sparkle with lively images, vivid examples, and down-to-earth, practical analogies.

In this book we have gathered together a few of Swami Kriyananda's similes, thoughts, and metaphors which we have found especially stimulating.* Our hope — indeed, our expectation — is that they will shed light on your own journey to an ever-deeper understanding of life. For man's comprehension must ever reach out toward limitlessness.

---

* Swami Kriyananda then edited them for inclusion in this book.
— The Publishers

1
Remain connected!

The farther a person tries to project his personal influence
beyond his own immediate concerns,
the more he inflates his ego.
In the end it may pop like a toy balloon,
becoming useless even to himself.
Perhaps this even explains certain cases of senility.

2
You are God's song

This world is like a symphony;
God is the great conductor
who alone can bring music out of everything.

3
Be a king

Master yourself:
In self-mastery alone lies true freedom!
You'll be able, then, to move about the world,
fearlessly, like a lion.

4
No one can own truth

Truth is one.
People try to slice it like a pie,
but even those slices
narrow to a point at the center.

5
Release your inner happiness

Be a divine lark:
Sing not to impress others,
nor to gain anything from them,
but for the sheer delight of singing.

6
Be a good gardener!

When cultivating your garden of life,
take care lest pride produce noxious weeds,
to choke and kill the wholesome plants
of devotion, kindness, and self-control.

7
Museum pieces

Theological definitions freeze truth
as if in blocks of ice.
Such careful formulae are like precious chinaware,
designed to be stored away safely,
and never brought out except on special occasions.
Experienced truth is for everyday use:
it breathes; it warms; it inspires.

8
Apply right principles

Freedom, when truly lived,
leads one forward on the path of law—of reality.
Every car driver knows that, though a car may
be steered from several positions,
it will steer best from the driver's seat.

9
Tune your mental radio

God, my Guru used to say,
is like a radio station;
His "programs" are broadcast on the "wavelength"
of superconsciousness.

10
Love God!

Without love, spiritual progress is
like walking with crutches.
It is slow work—and hard work, indeed!

11
Two sorts of happiness

The exhilaration of excitement stirs the mind,
but also befuddles it.
Seek that exhilaration which accompanies
calm upliftment—to the heart, especially.
People under the influence of excitement
jump up and down,
urged by upward spurts of energy in the spine.
Every leap upward, however, is followed by a descent.
Only heartfelt aspiration can take the mind
soaring at last, forever upward.

12

The currents of grace

As a bird in flight takes advantage of the air currents,
so try to ride on the currents of grace.
Be sensitive to them, for they will carry you
to success in everything.
Success is not always the outcome of stress:
Listen for whispered guidance in your soul.

13

Empty excitement

People think to inflate their happiness
with the "air" of false fulfillment.
The ego, however, punctures even valid undertakings
with the needle of pride,
and deflates them to insignificance.
Only when the balloon of happiness is attached
to the flow of inner joy
is true fulfillment found in everything.

14
Food for the heart

Were God never to nourish our hearts with His love, our very devotion for Him would become desiccated, like a river after years of no rain.

15
Moral and religious rigidity

People who cling too rigidly to religious dogmas reveal a lack of confidence in their beliefs!
They fear questioning lest their system of thought melt away like a snowman under a hot sun.

16
Gunfight

Every insult you hurl at others is like a boomerang: it will return, and wound you.

17

Illusion

The ego is like a sliver of glass in the sun:
Any light it emits only reflects
the sunlight of God's presence behind it.
The more one hides from that true light,
the less one can know of happiness,
and the more one must know of misery.

18

How important are we?

Our lives, like puffs of wind
on a handful of dust,
soon become nothing.
Don't base your self-definition on
what can never last.
Base it on your eternal reality, in God.

19

Mathematical certainty

Every fulfillment, sooner or later,
is cancelled out by a disappointment;
every success is replaced by a failure;
every joy must yield, in time, to sorrow;
every "up" is balanced by a "down."
Isn't it ironic that, after countless incarnations,
we never win a single game?
The sum total of all our striving always ends
in that final cipher: ZERO!

20

Clean your window!

Until you allow the Divine Light
to shine clearly through you,
your understanding will remain cloudy.
For your consciousness is like the colored pane
in a stained glass window.
If your pane is muddied over with impure desires,
the light of true understanding will be dimmed,
and the nature of your own, intrinsic glory
will be concealed under a gray layer of mediocrity.

21
Relationships

Lovingly tend every relationship,
like a garden,
until it yields the rich harvest of love.

22
Insensitivity

If you don't relate sensitively
to the world around you,
your life will be like a
violin string without a sounding board.
Separating you from broader realities,
life itself will become, for you,
but a thin screech.

23
Negativity

Avoid negativity like the disease it is;
it can infect all who keep their hearts open to it.
Negative thinking is evidence, truly, of satanic influence.

24

Outwardly, there is no escape

This world is like a deck of cards:
Shuffle it how you will,
the cards will change only in their sequence.
Instead of trying constantly
to make everything "come out all right,"
seek the ever-new joy of your own being.

25

Improving life on earth

Men often think by outward reforms
to bring radical improvement to humanity.
But see: man's problems continue.
And his troubles, like fleas,
accompany him everywhere.
Inner reform alone can improve human existence.

26
Change through revolution?

To try to improve the human lot
without transforming man inwardly
is like trying to strengthen a termite-ridden building
with a fresh coat of paint.

27
Cut the cords of attachment

Covetousness is like the ropes that tie
a balloon to the ground:
one's consciousness is prevented from soaring high
into skies of spiritual bliss.

28
Clarifying your vision

As an astronomer brings planets
into focus with his telescope,
so the yogi carefully brings
all his thoughts and aspirations to a focus
in the thought of God and His divine attributes.

29

Mastery

The true yogi moves and acts normally:
he talks, smiles, eats, and sleeps—
but always with a sense that he controls himself.
He never lets his emotions run away with him
like a car parked on a hill when the brakes fail.

30

Get a little rest!

The mind is like a donkey:
if you beat it constantly,
it will stop, and won't budge another step.
Give yourself time to rest a little.
Enjoy life. Relax occasionally,
when you feel the need.

31

Don't be an intelligent idiot!

Reality cannot be molded like play putty!
The greatest genius cannot make falsehood true.
Make it your first premise in life
to abide always by *what is*,
and not by what you wish things were.

32

Your personal filter

The ego wears colored glasses,
of which the tint is its desires.
The first step toward wisdom is
to remove those glasses and gaze on life impartially.

33

The secret of right understanding

Understanding comes by sympathy,
and still more by *empathy*.
As undampened notes on a piano will resonate
with the notes played on other instruments,
so kindness and generosity
remove the "damper" of egoism,
helping one to "resonate" with others
in their pains and difficulties.

34

Complexes

Insecurity, like a sponge,
sucks energy inward into itself.
Why take on the extra burden
of worrying about what others will think,
and of whether things will work or not?
Leave every result to its own destiny.
You can optimize that destiny by putting forth
your best efforts now.

35
Marriage

Marriage is a long-term investment.
Even when, tree-like, it grows
beyond the need for that kind of care
which must be lavished on a tender sapling,
such a close partnership nevertheless demands
special energy and careful, loving solicitude.

36
The death of love

Passivity in marriage becomes
a kind of slow-acting poison
which kills the plant of love.
Creativity, on the other hand, like a tonic,
can revive that plant, even if it is dying.

37
True vision

Revelation is wisdom,
and is distinct from intellectual understanding.
The intellect is like a child who,
after dismantling a watch,
works — ineffectually, as a rule —
to put the pieces back together again.

38
False understanding

To develop intuitive insight,
calm the feelings of your heart.
Else, without intuition,
one is like a man hopping down the street on one leg.

39
Inner guidance

The reasoning mind is like a ship without a rudder:
describing interesting patterns on the water,
but lacking any meaningful sense of direction.
True guidance comes from within;
it is rooted in superconscious awareness.

40
The danger of too much philosophizing

To what absurd heights philosophy can rise!—
high above the firm ground of objective reality,
soaring like a balloon with no ballast of common sense,
into heavens of abstract reasoning;
understanding soon perishes up there
for lack of life-sustaining oxygen.

41

Logic is unreliable

The most carefully constructed reasoning
has often collapsed like a house of cards
before the merest breeze
of some just-discovered or newly remembered fact!

42

Scriptural truth

God's truth is like a vast ocean
in which all the scriptures are mere drops.

43

Self-control

The mind is like a pail of milk which,
if riddled with the holes of restlessness, remains empty.
Any "milk" you pour into it
will all leak out again.

44

Intuition flourishes in calmness

Calm feeling is like a motionless lake.
The emotions are like ripples on the surface:
they distort the appearance of anything reflected there.
When the lake is without movement, however,
whatever is reflected in it appears as it truly is.

45

Spiritual progress

Spiritual progress should be
relaxed and natural, not forced.
Think of it as a growing tree
reaching out only gradually to touch a greater reality.
One reason for not judging others
is that one learns thereby not to judge oneself.
Remember: Nature never makes sudden leaps.

46

Peace

Peace isn't lying in wait for you over the next hill;
nor can it be constructed like a building,
brick by brick.
It must be part of the creative process itself.

47

You are part of the vastness of life

Accept reality as it is, and try to
harmonize yourself with it.
Truth, like Mohammed's mountain,
won't come to you: You must go to it.
In another sense, of course,
there is neither coming nor going:
the pilgrimage you must make is to plumb
your own inner depths.

48

Consciousness

Our *subconscious* is like the ocean floor,
with mountains, valleys, and broad plains.
Our *conscious* awareness is a protrusion
above the surface, like a little island.
The *superconscious* may be compared
to the heavens above us,
with their vast, alternating panoply
of daylight blue and shining stars at night.

49
Who am I?

The ego, like a wave on the ocean's surface,
is a manifestation, only, of a much deeper awareness
in Infinity.

50
Your private kingdom

Each of us is a kingdom of consciousness,
wherein each mind-citizen is a psychological trait,
possessing a life of its own.
Train your mental population to act harmoniously
by sending across the land
cool breezes of peace, harmony, and love.

51

Passing scenes

What you display of yourself outwardly
is not who or what you truly are.
You can express only aspects of
your potential for full consciousness—
like clouds in the sky,
whose display changes constantly.
People pass, over time, from sweetness to dryness
to callousness to bitterness to forgiveness
to love to inner happiness—
and on, to an unceasing procession
of other qualities and characteristics.
Always, however, whatever quality they manifest
is not their true Self.
At their center, eternally,
there remains that silent, watchful presence
which is the abiding reality of their being.

52

True understanding

Dogmatism is like still photography,
whereas true understanding is like cinematography;
it reveals the world in constant flux,
then shows change itself
as proceeding from a single beam of eternal light.

53

Don't be another King Canute!

Man thinks he can control his life,
but sees not that his overconfidence
is like Canute trying to prevent the tide
from rising on the shore.

54

Bathe yourself daily

Inner peace, like a weightless waterfall,
washes away all one's worries.
It bestows on him an ever-refreshing,
glad sense of confidence in his abilities.

55

Evolution

Life, like a lotus, rises
out of the mud of lower consciousness
toward, and finally into,
the light of divine awareness.

56

Courtesy

Courtesy is a healing balm;
it can soothe troubled hearts,
and win cooperation even from the hostile.

57

Your ideas

If you have what seems to you a good idea,
welcome suggestions concerning it, but protect it also,
like a tender plant, from anyone who,
like a bull running loose in a tulip field,
would trample on your enthusiasm.

58

Discrimination

Use discrimination like a sword:
With that sharp blade slice in two
whatever dilemma life places before you.
Separate right from wrong, truth from error,
and charity from cold insistence on rule and precedent.
Make the quest for joy your first priority.

59
Loyalty

Make loyalty the rudder of your barque of life.
If you stand firmly by high principles,
not even the strongest gales of wrong opinion
will be able to blow you off course.
Be loyal above all to truth
as you most deeply understand it.
You will then keep growing
in strength and understanding.

60
Attachment

Attachment, like an unripe fruit, clings
to whatever nourishes its hopes of fulfillment
even when fierce winds of tragedy buffet it.
Non-attachment, on the other hand, releases those hopes
at the very first breath of disappointment,
knowing that such is, indeed, the nature of this world.

61

The universal struggle

Every human being is, in a sense, a nation.
Human beings, like many countries,
are nations divided against themselves.
One segment of their "populace" affirms the right;
the other segment rejects that right,
and affirms the wrong.
Ask yourself at the end of every day:
Which side, this day, has won the battle?

62

Be the master of yourself

Every morning, command your subconscious
with some strong, wholesome affirmation.
Train your will to be a good general,
adamantly determined to fight for truth and right.
A military leader would be foolish
to forge ahead in the mere *hope*
that his army will follow him.
By affirmation, train your soldiers, also,
to be steadfastly obedient to your will.

63
Logic

Reason, like a railway train,
can follow only those tracks which lead outward
from already-existing premises.
Seek, rather, the inspiration of intuitive insight.

64
Leadership

An excellent way to run an organization
is to follow the ways of Nature.
As the human body submits to a chain of command
descending from the head,
a well-run institution is never so democratic
that it gives an equal voice to every member.
Leadership must seek support and consent from its followers,
but it needs, itself, to be competent,
experienced, and insightful.

65
Our bridge of ascension

Divine grace, like a ray of light,
is needed to illuminate the darkness of this world.
Only on rays of grace can we rise,
And only by so ascending
can we escape the dense fog of cosmic delusion.

66
Ariadne's wisdom

Like Ariadne's thread in the Greek myth of Theseus,
the ray of grace is our subtle tie to Higher Realities.
By following that thread, we can trace our way
out of the mind's labyrinth back to soul-freedom.

67
How to begin a project

Many a project has been started under
a burden of such carefully detailed plans
and weighty expectations that,
like an overloaded airplane,
it never manages to get off the ground.
Never, even during complicated projects,
lose touch with the flow of inner guidance.

68
Cultural stability

If a society never pauses to take stock of
the kind of world its members want their children to inherit,
the whole social framework may disintegrate, in time—
like a brick building without mortar.

69
Not "either . . . or"

Truth, like a diamond, is many-faceted.
Attempts to reduce it to dogmas
emphasize only the hardness, not the numerous facets.

70
Self-promotion

Among people of refinement,
self-promotion stands out like a badly tuned instrument
in a concert of chamber music.

71

Love injects life with wisdom

Reason without heart
may convince one, intellectually,
but it is like an autumn leaf—
perhaps beautiful, but for all that
lacking the sap of life.

72

Opinion vs. the truth

Truth is like the kernel of a nut:
opinion is the lifeless shell.
Truth, not opinion, is what we should respect.

73

When the equator is the goal

The first goal of life is equilibrium.
If the goal were to reach the equator, those north of it
would be told to go south, whereas
those living to the south
would be told to go north.
Human nature being what it is, those in each hemisphere
might well go farther after reaching their goal.
Those going south, then, would meet those coming north,
and cry, "Go back! You're supposed to go *south*!"
The others would cry, "No! No! we must all go *NORTH*!"
Thus may be explained most sectarian differences—
the curse of religion everywhere.

74

On dampening enthusiasm

Those who habitually discourage enthusiasm in others
kill them one little pinprick at a time.
Try to encourage people's good ideas.
If you can't sincerely give your support,
try to suggest alternatives.
Otherwise, remain silent.

75

Happiness

Happiness, like a plant, must be watered daily
with wholesome thoughts and beneficial action.

76

The loving heart

The heart is like the door of a building:
The air and light of truth can enter only
when the door is kept wide open.

77

Going within

Happiness is like an underground stream:
To find it, one must dig deep inside himself
with the tools of inner calmness
and acceptance of whatever *is*.

78

Live NOW!

Happiness is like a morning glory:
Yesterday's flower won't bloom again;
tomorrow's has yet to open.
Only today's flower can be fully enjoyed.

79

Developing intuition

Intuition can be developed by steady practice.
In this sense, like a muscle, it needs flexing.

80

Love, the great stimulator

Wisdom, without devotion, is like knowing
there is a good restaurant near where you live—
even knowing its entire menu—
but not being hungry enough to go there and eat.

81

Tethered goats!

We revolve our desires ceaselessly around the ego.
The mind, like a tethered goat,
is firmly tied to the post of selfhood.
Man will never truly enjoy a broader reality
so long as he clings to the thought of "I."

82

Let it flow!

The energy in every human relationship
is like flowing water:
As long as there is creative input,
the relationship will remain fresh.

83

True security

The wise have ever said that one should place his
full trust only in God.
To rely too much on outer circumstances
is like expecting stability of a ship at sea.

84

For men especially:

Until the intellect is softened by heartfelt tenderness,
it is like earth without water:
weighty, but infertile.

85

For women especially:

Until the heart's feelings
can accept willingly the guidance of calm reason,
they will again and again shatter life's edifice —
like a brick building in an earthquake.

86
Peaceless

My Guru used to say:
The mind of the worldly man is like a sieve,
riddled with desires, worries, and distractions.
It is impossible for such a person
to gather and hold the milk of peace.

87
Question yourself

"To be willing to doubt one's own first principles
is the mark of a civilized man."
So has it been rightly said.
By contrast, to hold to a belief dogmatically
is like saying,
"This much I will have of truth, and no more."
Be firm in your principles, but never be rigid.

88
The lamp of true insight

In deep spiritual matters, to expect theologians
to shed light in the dark corners of truth
is like expecting a diver
to illuminate the ocean depths
with a keychain flashlight.

89
How to handle desires

To seek release from desire by indulging it
is like placing wood on an already-raging fire
in the hope of quenching its flames.

90
First, be true to yourself

Inner peace is like oil:
It lubricates the machinery of life,
and enables everything to function smoothly.

91
Ego-investment

The average person, lacking inner balance,
behaves like an eccentric flywheel:
The faster he spins with desires,
the more violently his mind vibrates
until his very hold on life flies apart.

92

What, exactly, is truth?

Enlightenment is like peeling an onion.
Once one removes the last layer of ego-identity,
he finds himself in a huge, empty chamber;
for the ego consists of nothing but layers of self-definition.
Into that vast, empty chamber, however,
Infinity will then enter with soft tread,
bearing the lantern of Eternal Bliss.

93

All true paths express the same Light

Like the seven colors of a rainbow,
so the spectrum of reality has many aspects,
none of them better or worse than any other.
Each fulfills some special need.

94

Siamese twins

Sorrow is the sigh that succeeds every emotional joy.
Joy's full-throated euphoria
is like the dawn after a long night of sorrow.
Duality swings constantly, like a pendulum,
back and forth between eternal opposites.
The secret of lasting happiness
is to seek rest at the center,
and not to let your feelings swing back and forth
in constant reaction to outer circumstances.

95

Powerful help

The guru is like a strong river
which draws into itself every sluggish eddy,
making one's entire flow of energy and consciousness
pure and powerful.

96

The best teacher

A divine incarnation is like a graduate
who returns to the university where he once studied
to offer, from his own experience,
help, guidance, and encouragement
to those who are still undergraduates.

97

Shame is not expiation

To burden oneself with blame
is like a drowning man
asking for a heavy stone.
You are not your mistakes!

98

For the youth

Adolescence needs a cause—
or, better still, an abundance of causes.
It needs something to do.
It is like dynamite: If exploded above the ground,
it may disrupt or destroy;
but if it is first placed carefully in the earth,
it may help in the building of highways
over which, someday, many vehicles will pass.

99

Let light enter your home

Divine grace is like the sunlight shining on a building:
it enters fully into those rooms
where the curtains are opened wide.

100

Karma

The karmic burden people carry
is like the sheet of ice on a large lake.
To break that whole sheet at once would be impossible;
by drilling at one spot, however,
one can easily penetrate through the ice
to the body of water underneath.
Even so, by going to your own center in meditation,
you can pass through the ice field of karma
to merge back into the great lake of God's consciousness.
His love will then help you to melt the entire field.

101

The need for a guru

As long as your awareness is centered in selfhood,
you won't be able to disavow the ego altogether—
even as one cannot overcome seasickness
during a raging storm
while tossing helplessly in a rowboat.
This is why one needs the inner guidance of a true guru.

102
Two legs are needed!

Both science and art are necessary.
Science is the methodology;
art is intuitive perception.
Each one, without the other,
is like trying to run on only one leg.

103
Perseverance

A person who starts things eagerly,
but doesn't follow through on them,
is like someone who tries to create a bonfire
on the bare ground with one newspaper.

104
Your inner "Jordan"

The spine, like a river,
channels currents of energy constantly between body and brain.
An increased awareness of those currents
leads to divine awakening.

105

Global transformation

Our earth needs help desperately.
To try to save it, however, by rescuing a few trees
is like putting a band-aid on a just-amputated limb.
Much more is needed!
The greatest good you can do for our planet
is to try, by words and example,
to uplift the over-all level of consciousness.

106

Worldly recognition

The applause of multitudes is like ocean surf:
effervescent, briefly stimulating, and evanescent.
Better a scolding from the wise
than the adulation of fools.

107

Control your reactions

How others behave toward you
is, like the weather, beyond your control.
How *you* behave toward them, however,
and the direction of your own feelings,
need be determined only by yourself.

108

Be always sincere

Cleverness, like stylish clothing,
is useless if it covers only a corpse.

109

Emotions vs. divine inspiration

The stimulation one feels from a strong emotion
is like the stronger flow of water
one gets from a hose by squeezing the tip.
A much greater surge of power comes, however,
from holding one's awareness up to the superconscious,
and seeking higher guidance and support.

110

Spiritual communities

Spiritual communities are living laboratories,
wherein values are tested and proved,
wrong attitudes clearly revealed for what they are,
and right ones justified by visible results.
People who live for God and help one another
are seen to be always happy,
and those who live selfishly are never happy.

111

The mind's little bucket

Man imagines himself capable of
understanding everything by the intellect alone.
In this presumption he is like St. Augustine
in the story of a little child
who appeared to him one day on a beach and said,
"Are you trying to empty the whole sea
with that little 'bucket' of your mind?"
(Having spoken those words, the child disappeared!)

112

The guru

The guru is like a magnet.
The mental tendencies of most people,
like the molecules in an ordinary bar of steel,
are turned at random, their polarity neutralized.
Those tendencies, in the presence of an enlightened sage,
become gradually aligned in a single direction:
upward, toward the brain.

113

What is good art?

A work of art, like conversation, should communicate.
It should try to convey clearly and well
what one wants to say,
and ought not merely to stimulate people's appreciation
for form and color.

114

The art of happy living

Life's joys are like quicksilver:
Tighten your grip on them, and they will fly from your grasp.
To hold on to happiness, simply receive it,
as it were in the cup of your hand.
Don't clutch it with attachment.

115

Concentration equals power

Concentration is like focusing diffused rays of light
into a single, laser-like beam.
Such mental focus bestows power to succeed at anything.

116

Entering the New Age

At present, mankind is like a growing adolescent
whose clothes are bursting at the seams.
Old institutions and attitudes—
legacies from the past—are too narrow
to accommodate the expansive spirit of this era.

117

Empty laughter

Joy, if it lacks a sense of higher truth,
is, like drunken jollity, muddled and confused.

118

Refer back to first principles

Formal reasoning is like tuning a piano
by first adjusting the D note to the C;
the E note to the D;
the F to the E; and so on up the scale,
relating each note only to the one just before it,
but not also to the first note.
After progressing only a little distance,
one will find the last note incorrectly tuned to the first:
Undetectable variations, increasing by minute degrees,
will soon result in an outright dissonance.
To avoid this progressive error,
a piano tuner refers back repeatedly to his first note.
So also must reason check back repeatedly
with its first premise.

119

Clear your inner channels of perception

Attachment and desire are like radio static:
they prevent the clear reception
of any insights one wants to achieve.

120

Troublesome emotions

Likes and dislikes are like troublesome neighbors,
who rob us of our inner peace.
Extreme feelings plunge one into a whirlpool,
tossing him about helplessly.
In time, they can drown us in delusion.

121

Castles of sand

Even though material fulfillment can bring
quick satisfaction,
it is like a wall constructed of sand and gravel,
but with too little bonding cement:
it quickly crumbles, to become mere rubble.

122

Achieve true perceptions

Emotional understanding is like the scenes
caught by the click of a camera shutter.
The still images are preserved on paper,
but the scene itself quickly changes,
and whatever perception one feels he has gained
vanishes as though it had never been.

123

Aspiring to the heights

Many spiritual aspirants equate success
with achievements that fall short of oneness with God.
Such seekers are like a mountain climber
who is content to climb a moderately high peak,
when Everest, the highest of them all, towers nearby.
In their souls, they will never rest
until they have conquered the final peak
of union with their own true Self.

124

Human vs. soul power

The thoughts produced by human reason are like
heavy trucks, shifting gears downward every time
they lumber up a little grade of rational difficulty.
On higher levels of consciousness,
the mind soars like a bird,
high above even the mountain peaks of difficulties.

125
God loves us

Carefully chiseled-out prayers are like petitions
submitted to a throned emperor—
uttered in anxious fear of being rejected.
God doesn't want our diplomacy.
He is our Nearest and Dearest:
He is our very own.
He wants from us only our confiding love.

126
The key of life

Time is spherical; its beginnings and endings
are mere projections of thought.
Like grains of sand in an hourglass,
we pass through, and when a cycle is finished and
the hourglass is turned, we pass through again.
To solve the riddle of our existence,
we must withdraw from egoic involvement,
and simply watch the process.

127
The wisdom of the heart

We cannot calm the waves of emotion
by suppressing them,
but only by inspiring them to love stillness.

128
The other side of the moon

Religion itself has two sides,
as do all things in Creation.
In religion, there is its outer aspect:
recognized and enshrined in sacred structures everywhere.
The inner aspect is like the other side of the moon,
hidden from egoic gaze, but revealed
to the soul when experienced in meditation.
"And ye shall seek me, and find me,
 when ye shall seek for me with all your heart." (Jer. 29:13)

129

The circle: a new concept for understanding

The essential truth in all religions is one,
like the center of a circle.
The search for that center is, in every religion,
the *Way of Awakening*.
The paths outward from that center, on the contrary,
are the *Ways of Belief*.
The farther they move in all directions,
the more separate and alone they become.

130

Religious unity

Once divine aspiration is seen to exist everywhere,
religious differences only increase our appreciation
for Truth in all its manifestations.
See how beautiful is a crystal,
when turned to let light illuminate it from different angles,
such that, seen one way, it is red;
seen another way, it is orange, or yellow—
green, blue, indigo, violet.
The future of religion lies in the direction of unity
in the single, grand concept: Self-realization.

131

Seek lasting realities

Fads of the moment are like waves:
rising, falling—and, at last, forgotten altogether.
Seek values in life that never change.

132

Shells of ego

We are like chicks facing the task
of breaking out of our little shells of ego—
out of our habitual ways of looking at and doing things;
out of our social conditioning—
and of seeing that we are part of an infinite reality!

133

Opposites

Most works of art are like lighter-than-water pyramids
floating, inverted, on the sea:
Their base is exposed at surface,
but the deeper one probes them for meaning,
the less substance one finds.
Great works of art, by contrast, having weight,
show only their tip at the surface:
The deeper they are probed, however,
the more meaning they are seen to contain,
for they are based in eternal truth.

134

The one element

Ideas are like ice floes on a river.
As ice is composed of the same element
as the water on which it floats,
so our ideas are made of the same element, consciousness.
Let our minds flow with the stream of consciousness,
and not lie frozen in lumps of dogma at the surface,

135

Unitive vision

All living beings, all things, all thoughts,
all emotions, all inspirations
are like ocean waves:
endlessly varied, yet forever rising from
only one reality.

136

The great delusion

Our egos are like little jets of flame on a gas burner;
each one having the appearance of individuality,
but each in fact but a manifestation
of the unifying gas underneath.

137

Scientific pride

Most scientists, lacking superconscious intuition,
are like the artist who, beholding a beautiful sunset,
boasted, "I could paint a better sunset than that!"

138

Be contented with less

Desires are like openings in a dam:
They empty the heart's lake of its
waters of happiness.

139

Think, before you speak

As notes played on a violin can either please or grate,
depending on how the instrument is played,
so words can either please or offend,
depending on the consideration, or lack of it,
with which they are uttered.
Be careful always to speak kindly and sympathetically.
Even when scolding, endeavor never to hurt.

140

Truth, not cleverness, is what wins

Victories that are won by cleverness
are like mist on a river:
They evaporate, and what remains is only flowing water.

141

Reflections everywhere!

People mirror back to you
the feelings you express toward them.
If you want to be liked,
first of all, show others that you like them.

142

Seeking importance?

Dreams of self-importance
are like soap bubbles in the sun:
colorful, but empty and evanescent.

143

Advice for meditation

Never end a meditation
with the meditation techniques you practice.
These are like finger exercises on a piano:
They enable one to play fluently,
but cannot replace actual music.
Once, through the practice of techniques,
your mind has become focused and quiet,
offer it up in stillness
to the inflow of divine inspiration.

144

The divine reality

God, the Supreme Spirit,
is like an ocean in relation to which
all manifested forms of creation
are only wave-vibrations.

145

Alexander the Great

The intricacies of karma are such
that no amount of outward effort can unravel them.
The mythical Gordian knot could not be untied,
for even if one strand was loosened,
in that very act, another one was tightened.
Alexander "the Great" cut that knot with one blow.
Even so, we may rid ourselves of all karma forever
by cutting our own Gordian knot with the sword of calmness,
forged in loving meditation
to the sharpness of keen discrimination.
In calm detachment, offer up your past actions
to inner freedom in God.
Tell yourself: "He alone is the doer of everything!"

146

First develop inner clarity

Too many people are like enthusiastic viewers
at an art exhibition,
who pass hurriedly from one painting to another,
so fearful of missing any,
that they miss the message in all of them!

147

Misty weather

The minds of most people are like cloudy skies.
Their mental clouds sometimes part briefly,
and let in the sunlight of clarity,
but too soon they re-form
as the mists of past karma again hide the sun.
Let us rid our own skies of every cloud,
that we may see clearly once more the sun of truth.

148

Restless happiness

Worldly people are like those nightclub-goers
who love noise and glitter,
but who become uneasy if asked to contemplate
the calm beauty of a moonlit lake.

149

Divine grace

Divine grace flows through human nature
as water flows through a hose.
Keep straight the hose of your aspiration,
that grace may flow through it unimpeded.

150

Leadership is an art

A clumsy leader is like an untrained singer
who bellows to hide his inability to produce a pure tone.
He is like a bad actor
who bludgeons his audience with bombast
because he is unable to win them with subtlety.
He is like the mechanic who, unable to find
the malfunction in a motor,
kicks it in the hope of starting something.
Every tailor knows you can't jam a thread roughly
through the eye of a needle.

151
Peaceful attunement

Most people, like bad musicians,
don't even hear sour notes in themselves.
Their interaction with others produces only discord.
Meditation is the way to fine-tune the human instrument.

152
The true road to reform

The most beneficial changes cannot be legislated:
They must grow naturally, like grass roots,
out of the common understanding.
Governments cannot set the moral tone for an age,
but can only reflect back to the people
what the people themselves accept as true.
Beneficial changes can only be inspired by individuals.

153

The waves of ego

The higher one's wave of egoism,
the more it sets itself in competition with other egos,
all of whom protrude far above their base in God.
In consequence, they live together in constant stress and fear.
Seek, rather, to be a little ripple:
close to the ocean of divine awareness.
Tell yourself, "I am only a ripple on God's ocean,
at peace with all my brothers and sisters around me."

154

Be even-minded

Many people confuse progress with mere change.
The more excitement they stir up like dust,
the more productive they imagine themselves!
Such people "progress" like jeeps bouncing over rough terrain,
their movement almost as much vertical as it is horizontal.
Seek steady progress, rather. Don't move in excited jerks.

155
Face life's trials

Trials are like dogs:
They lose heart when we confront them,
but give eager chase the moment we turn and flee.

156
Desires are like wrapping paper

Happiness cannot be found in mere things.
As one wraps a gift to make it more attractive,
so people "wrap" the objects of their desire
in colorful, bright expectations.
When those desires are "unwrapped," however—
that is to say, fulfilled—
they never give lasting satisfaction,
and often disappoint from the beginning:
How dull they seem, beside their shiny covering!

157

False promises

Desires are like those tin cans that proclaim to tourists:
"Air from Capri, Italy!" or,
"Air from Yosemite Valley!"
By the time one breathes that air,
it has already mingled with the smog all around it!
The promised fulfillment is only a bright expectation
wrapped around emptiness.

158

The hidden power

Inspiration is its own reality;
so also is the upliftment it conveys.
The thoughts it suggests may vary in appearance,
like colored lights on a Christmas tree,
but the electric power behind them never varies.
Their differences lie only in their shape and color.
Conscious Bliss, like those lights, is ever new,
but even so is the same always,
and the insights it can inspire assume countless forms:
mathematical, poetic, musical—even culinary!

159

What most people don't know

The more one revels in outer pleasure,
the more he must experience also its opposite pain.
Oppositional states swing back and forth,
like pendulums.
The farther their movement in either direction,
the farther must be its opposite movement.
Wise is he who seeks satisfaction at his own center:
in the Self, within.

160

The different paths of religion

Truth can be expressed in countless ways.
In this respect, it is like leaves on a single tree:
though generically they are all the same,
each one is unique in its appearance.

161
We got lost

Every human being desires a love
that will lead to perfect bliss.
It could not be otherwise,
for all of us, like Prodigal Sons,
emerged long ago to roam in foreign territory,
far from our bliss-home in God.

162
Keep your love steadfast

Keep your love ever central, like the sun.
Witness the planets of fleeting experiences
which, in the vastness of time and space,
rotate around you, and draw life from your love.

163
Say YES to life!

Keep your heart open, like flower petals,
to the sun of life's experiences.
Man has much to learn, even from tragic tests;
The light may sometimes scorch,
but it can also burn away one's imperfections.

164

A meditative practice

Offer gifts of love upward from your heart,
and outward, through the point between the eyebrows.
Such gifts, like upward-soaring flames
from an all-purifying fire,
are life-transforming — for both you and others.

165

Warmth from your heart

Be like the sunlight:
offer life, healing, and encouragement to all.

166

Be strong in your friendship

In your loyalty to others, be like the oak tree
which, though buffeted by high winds,
never ceases to provide sheltering shade.

167

Time and timelessness

If you want to be creative,
concentrate on flowing motion
rather than on the countless problems along the way.

168

Right attitude

For attunement with God,
right attitude is necessary,
as a radio listener, who desires a particular wavelength,
takes care to turn his dial sensitively.
Even so, right attitude will help
in attuning your mind to higher consciousness.

169
To realize your dream

How common it has been through the ages
for people to consider God impossibly distant, like the moon!
And how few, accepting scriptural testimony,
combined with the longing of their own souls,
have looked higher than this world's dusty marketplace,
and have sought communion with Him.
What these few have found
is that His distance lies only in men's thoughts!

170
Seek truth as a unity

There are certain teachings that lie,
like the ocean depths,
beneath the dancing waves of mere words and ideas.
Seek below that surface froth.
Be concerned, rather, with seeking sunken treasure!

171
The flash of revelation

Revelation goes beyond mere logical conviction:
it conveys deep, absolute certainty.
It is not the conclusion of some long thought process,
but, rather, arrives fully developed—
like Athena from the brow of Zeus.

172
Attunement

For those to whom the deepest reality of life is God,
everything manifests Him, as every river flows to the sea.
Every thought, then, is infused with bliss.

173
How to account for Creation

Vibrations refer back repeatedly to a central point,
like the tines of a tuning fork, which move left and right
from a point of rest at the center.
Ocean waves rise and fall, but no matter how high a wave,
the level of the ocean itself never changes.
Similarly, God vibrated a part of His consciousness
from that calm center of Absolute Calmness,
to produce the appearance of everything we call Creation.

174

Divine Omnipresence

Like a thread which passes through a necklace,
uniting all the beads,
so the divine consciousness
runs through all things, bringing them unity.
In God, everything is one.

175

An empty promise

This world, so bright with promises,
is like the dewdrop that glistens on a rose at dawn.
Its message is of lasting beauty,
but it speaks false.
The drop soon disappears in vapor.
And where does the vapor go?
It rises toward the sun.
Human aspirations rise, also,
seeking to merge with the "sun" of Perfect Bliss.

176
Never close your heart

Under the blows of adversity
man tends to close himself, inwardly,
like a traveler before the fierce onslaught
of desert storms;
like the tortoise which, at any threat to its safety,
withdraws protectively into its shell;
or like the rabbit, which withdraws into its warren
from all approaching danger:
we see that this self-protective tendency is universal.
Have the courage to resist it —
to hold your heart ready to receive
God's unceasing reassurance and support,
and never to close yourself in from whatever *is*.

177

Is anyone "chosen of God"?

Divine grace is impersonal; it is not, like man's will,
dependent on taste and inclinations.
Grace has no favorites: it shines impartially everywhere,
like the sunlight.
"God chooses those," my Guru used to say,
"who choose Him."
Be confident that you are always God's very own.

178

The Divine Promise

Like the stars in the sky, God is always there.
As in daylight, however, those little points
of nocturnal assurance become invisible,
so when the ego is active
it blots out one's awareness of God's presence.
Still, it shines always within us.
Though we see Him not, He is ever there.

179

The non-school

The spiritual path is a school. In one respect, however,
it is unlike the schooling of this world,
for here one goes to school so as to learn,
but the goal of meditation is to *un*learn:
to rid oneself of those things which define him falsely.
What we all are is the eternal, ever-changeless Spirit.

180

Creativity

Any slight lack of clarity at the source of a creative act
may result in a mixed message at the end.
For, like the generations in a tape recording,
each successive copy of which slightly reduces the fidelity,
so in the creative process, if any loss of energy occurs,
whether in the editing or in the process of production,
there will be a loss of fidelity to the original purpose.

181

Adapting art to inner realities

Curves, not straight lines,
are more natural in the expression of higher truths;
maturity brings smoothness and roundness to expression,
as it does to pebbles on a riverbed.
Sharp angles in art suggest immaturity:
the delusion that one can conquer nature's laws,
or bend them to man's will.

182

Energy generates magnetism

A strong flow of energy in the body
is like the flow of electricity through a copper wire:
It generates a magnetic field.
Inspiration can actually be attracted by will power:
The greater the flow of energy directed by the will,
the more quickly a solution will be reached.
Low-keyed deliberations, on the other hand,
even after months of weighty discussion,
never produce anything but halfhearted compromise.

183
Self-interest equals disinterest

Self-interest in any relationship
is like placing the same poles of two magnets too close together:
Instead of increasing the attraction between them, they repel.
Hence the popular saying, "Familiarity breeds contempt."

184
Look beyond form

When we love others, our love passes like the wind
through their outer covering,
and reaches the reality within them.

185
True laughter is inwardly watchful

At any average cocktail party, watch those present:
see how desperately they are trying to have a good time!
Such merriment is like the drinks they hold in their hands:
a kind of drug, the main benefit of which is
that it induces forgetfulness.
Be attentive always, and calmly watchful—
not so much of others as of yourself.

186
Be inwardly free

Grieve not when the winds of circumstance
wrest you, like an autumn leaf,
from your accustomed security.
That disruption may prove only to be
the first step toward greater accomplishment.
Dead leaves, moreover, may help to fertilize the ground
for future crops!

187
Surface reassurances

Some people are like the hostess at a dinner party
who smiles at the guests
while giving her husband a well-aimed kick under the table!
Be openly sincere with others,
and they will always meet you kindly.

188

Words of hope

Often when hope is darkest,
your life, like the night-veiled sky,
is only preparing for the dawn.

189

Be protective of your inner freedom

The bear is free to enter a trap or to stay out of it:
Only if he stays out, however, will he keep his freedom.
Similar is it with human beings:
Man is free to embrace delusion or to reject it.
If he cooperates with his true, higher nature,
he will remain free.
If, however, he follows the dictates of desire,
those very desires will constitute his imprisonment.

190

A perspective

In modern society, the trend I see for the future
is toward a growing demand for quality over quantity.
This shift will include a new focus on the *inner* Self.
Science says, "The electron is the key to the universe."
Man will come in time to say, "The key to understanding
is my own self!"

191

Einstein's revolution

Einstein declared that matter is energy in vibration.
His discovery, however, did not relegate matter
to nonexistence.
It has only meant that there is more to matter
than first appeared.
Matter has now been exalted—like the peasant boy of fable
who was found to have the talent of a great artist.

192

Superconscious powerhouse

The superconscious represents much higher awareness
than the conscious mind.
It is, in fact, the true source of *all* awareness.
The conscious and subconscious minds filter that awareness—
stepping it down, so to speak, like a transformer,
to an intensity that will be acceptable in our homes.

193

Inner disturbances during meditation

Don't be like a weak swimmer—
easily swept away by a strong tide.
Devotion, and attunement with the guru,
can give you the strength
to swim against the worst tides of karma.

194

Yoga positions for the mind

The mind, like the body, can ossify.
Stretch it frequently, to keep it limber.
Welcome new ideas; develop them; ask yourself,
do they lead to further conclusions?

195

Be inwardly relaxed

Deep concentration is possible only
in a state of relaxation.
Tension, physical or mental, divides
one's commitment of energy—
like that loose filament which prevents a thread
from penetrating the eye of a needle.

196

The answer to doubt

Spiritual doubts cannot be resolved, finally,
by thought or argument.
Every question answered only leads to a hundred more.
Doubt is like a tree which, though felled,
produced a forest.
The tree of doubt, though cut to its roots by good answers,
will lie on the "forest floor" of intellectuality,
waiting for further doubts to grow and flourish again.
Doubting is above all a state of consciousness.
The only way out of it, finally, is to love.

197

Creative expansion

The secret of life's development
lies not at its periphery, but at its center.
Everything in Nature expands outward from that center.
Whatever you yourself create,
seek to expand the little germ of inspiration you've felt
outward from its center to its own natural limits.

198

Center everywhere, circumference nowhere

Every point of space is the hub of its own wheel:
its influences, like spokes, radiate outward in all directions.
Indeed, a better analogy—
though one perhaps more difficult to comprehend—
would be an expanding sphere,
with rays of light shooting out from it
in all directions to infinity.
Every point in the universe radiates its special point of view,
from which all else can be explained.
Every perception is also in some way unique:
One truth in everything,
and all things contained in each expression of truth.

199

Living with high ideals

The concept, "Cities of Light," might be likened to a wheel,
the hub of which is the concept itself:
a life lived in ever-expanding awareness.
Spokes from that hub are the activities;
the rim, which encloses the communal life as a totality,
represents the point of contact with the outer world.
The hub, and the awareness it generates,
comprise its heart, and its real strength.

200

Aristotelean logic

The Western view of reality is like a tennis match:
truth on one side, falsehood on the other,
forever divided by a fixed net.
Real life, however, consists of *directions*,
never of fixed positions.
Let your direction be ever upward, toward truth.

201

Be grounded, when presenting truth

Truth, when presented rightly, is like a pyramid:
its base rising, through increasingly refined understanding,
to a pinnacle.
If the pyramid is inverted to rest on its tip,
any challenge will knock it over.
Never try to balance your edifice of ideas
on one little point of perception!
Broaden your base with as many facts as possible.

202

Life is a movie

A cinema creates its illusion of reality
by mixing together shadows, light, and color
in endless variety.
In life, similarly, remember that change
is but a projection of the one light
in the projector.
To the enlightened sage,
there is but one light radiating outward
from inside the countless centers of space itself.

203

Be a divine sculptor

God created us not by molding us, like sculpture.
He *became* us, as we ourselves "become"
our own dreams at night.
As those dreams appear real,
but vanish when we awake,
so when our own consciousness is withdrawn, at death,
our bodies simply cease to exist;
their atoms re-coalesce in new forms.
And when we achieve oneness with God,
our human self and its defining characteristics will disappear,
and only the memory of us will remain—
that, and our influence,
by which we can still touch the lives of others.

204

Three bodies enclose the soul

This image is one offered by my Guru:
Imagine, he said, a bottle floating on the sea.
That bottle represents your physical body.
That bottle, however, encloses another "bottle":
the astral body;
and within that bottle there is still another one:
the causal body.
The soul, like a drop of water, is enclosed
in the inmost bottle;
it cannot merge back into the ocean
until its last remaining enclosure, the causal body,
has been broken by deepest realization.
Only then can it merge back into God.

205

Deepen your awareness

Our subtle energies are powerful and important.
Compared to electricity they may seem weak,
but their source is limitless.
The energy in our bodies has its roots in Infinity.
Reality in its subtler aspects has power over the grosser.

206
Success

A rheostat, by limiting the flow of electricity,
softens the lighting in a room.
The natural voltage, however, is not lessened.
Many people try to increase their "mental voltage"
by straining, as though the mind were a muscle.
Their sense of strain is evident in their furrowed foreheads
and their fiercely knitted eyebrows.
Such strain is counterproductive.
Relaxation, faith, and a determinedly happy attitude
would carry them to supreme success in everything.

207
Are you afraid of expanded realities?

Man's ego dreads the thought of infinity.
His fear may be compared to the timidity of a caged bird,
which cannot imagine itself in flight.
Once it discovers its real nature, however,
it soars in joyous freedom to the sky.
Your soul was meant to soar high
through skies of Cosmic Bliss.

208

The purpose is the same

Spiritual upliftment has little or nothing to do
with being a Hindu, Christian, Moslem, Buddhist, or Jew.
As people, after a good meal, feel contented in their repletion,
whether they ate curry, pasta, or paella,
even so, prayers to Allah, Buddha, or Jehovah
serve the purpose only of opening windows
onto the inner flow of God's Bliss.

209

The true guide

If a person is fortunate enough to have
a true guide on the path,
let him, in God's name, repose complete faith in him or her.
For only such a one can, like Moses,
lead us out of servitude in Pharaoh's land—
where all is humiliation and defeat—
to cosmic freedom in the Self.

210

Many images: one Source

Egoic self-awareness may be compared
to the moon's reflection in a pot of water:
as many egos, so many pots.
Each pot contains the same substance, water.
Each reflection seems individual.
Yet they are all but images of the same one moon.

211

Complete your painting!

Life evolves to ever-higher levels of awareness;
this fact means that the higher *potentials* awaiting us
are our own *central* reality:
We already *are* that which we seek.
What we see are the first tentative lines on the canvas,
which represent the unfolding purpose in our souls.
In this respect, we should try to be God-like:
never stopping until our work of self-transformation is complete,
and we find ourselves the bliss for which we've always longed.

212
The newest scientific findings

We face the need today to adjust our minds
to thinking more in terms of movement
than of static positions.
We have tried for too long to freeze reality
in fixed forms and dogmas.
The transition to this new perception may be compared
to a shift away from still photography to cinematography
as man's understanding embraces greater motility.

213
The calm experience of saints

To a calmly uplifted, expanded consciousness,
the stresses and anguish of ordinary life
seem only ripples on a limitless, deep ocean.

214
Satan's role is, inherently, divine

Satan is the villain in the cosmic drama;
He has no separate reality of his own.
His function is to lend interest and meaning to the show.
He is necessary to the story line,
for without him man would never learn discrimination.
We would never turn away from hatred and indifference to love,
nor would we ever rise out of the mud of worldly involvement
into the freedom of cosmic happiness.
The very misery Satan causes is a necessary prod;
it keeps us struggling toward final soul liberation.

215
You are beautiful

Your individuality is like a light bulb:
Though you seem to shine on your own,
your light derives from a higher source.

216

Distorted harmonies

The ego-centered individual is like a musician
who plays his own interpretation of the music,
ignoring the orchestra of which he is a member.
Realize that you are part of a greater reality.
The more you emphasize your own separateness,
the greater the distortion you will introduce
into the over-all harmony.

217

The staircase

Spiritual evolution is like climbing a long spiral staircase.
The ego, as it mounts upward,
grows increasingly aware that it has a higher potential
to accomplish effortlessly all it needs
by sensitive attunement to higher truths,
than by trying painstakingly
to figure out everything for itself.

218

A secret of success

The pathway of spiritual attainment is the spine,
which is like a bar magnet of which the molecules are aligned
in a north-south direction:
the larger the number of molecules so aligned,
the stronger the magnetism.
In human beings, the seeds of
outward desires and mental tendencies lie dormant,
buried in the spine as little vortices of energy, ready to sprout.
The more their sprouting energy is aligned—
that is, directed upward toward the brain—
the stronger their magnetism
to attract material success, good health,
and divine bliss.

219

Reaction and involvement

We receive impressions passively at first,
before we see the need for action concerning them.
Next, we react, perhaps with interest,
experiencing likes and dislikes, desires and aversions,
making those impressions part of our reality.
Emotional reactions are binding on our consciousness.
(We cringe, for example, if a violinist plays off key,
and wish he would find the right pitch.)
If things go wrong for us, we try to correct them.
Mentally involving ourselves in the scenes around us,
we approve or disapprove endlessly.
By such involvement, we entangle ourselves karmically.
When, with spiritual advancement,
we discover the need to become *dis*entangled from the great web
in which too many find themselves ensnared,
we find at last only one solution:
We must trace our awareness back, seeing each impression
as having been merely introduced to our perception from outside:
never did it have anything to do with our true inner reality.
The road to freedom leads progressively back
from outer involvements to centeredness in the Self.

220
Releasing the balloon of aspiration

Spiritual progress may be compared to a helium-filled balloon,
the ascent of which is natural, and can be prevented only
by ropes, or hindered by heavy ballast.
Devotion and divine aspiration lift one naturally
toward our one source, in God.
Worldly desires and attachments, and the habit they induce
of directing our flow of energy outward,
resist the upward flow of soul aspiration.
Effort on the spiritual path may be likened
to cutting the ropes which hold the balloon to the ground,
and pushing out from our basket of self-definitions
all the ballast of self-involvement.

221
Your past actions need not touch you

Individual karmas follow us like the wake of a ship:
In themselves they have no reality,
but are only disturbances on the ocean of awareness.
Karma can be neutralized by dispassion,
or ignored by rising high above it
on wings of divine devotion.

222

Your choice of how to live

A person who lives only to gratify his physical desires
is hardly more than a beast of burden.
The load he carries is composed of accumulated cares.
He eats, sleeps, breeds, and dies:
Meanwhile, his entire contribution to the world
is hardly more than that of a crocodile asleep on a riverbank!
Remember this, O angel of power,
light, and potential for highest accomplishment!
You were born to embrace the universe!

223

The role of saints

The Supreme Spirit seldom intervenes directly
in the affairs of man.
God may be compared to a power station,
the voltage of which must be stepped down
before it can enter people's homes.
Such is the role played by saints,
who bring God's power and wisdom to mankind.

224
The mystery of time

Time is a mental concept.
The events through which we pass
are like the pages of a book:
whether present, remembered, or anticipated,
as the story unfolds to our awareness.
Were we able to look ahead
and see what the future holds for us,
we might not feel up to facing those challenges.
If, however, we remove ourselves a little
from mental involvement in the action,
we may see another reality:
Here we sit, calmly reading! In our eternal reality,
there is no past, present, and future:
these all exist simultaneously.
There is only the Eternal Now.

225
Our rough edges

Association with others might be compared to
pebbles rolling together down a riverbed,
gradually rubbing against one another until
their rough edges become smooth.

226
Delusion's vicious cycle

Nervous people fidget constantly—
a sign that their nervous systems are disordered.
Look for outward symptoms of any mental state.
Note how each state feeds on itself:
nervousness, if not resisted, leads to *increased* nervousness.
Anger, if outwardly expressed, brings but temporary relief—
followed by still-greater anger.
It is like the feedback that occurs
when a microphone and a loudspeaker
are turned to face each other.
Never seek release (except temporarily, in order to retrench)
by further indulging a desire.
Seek freedom by inner non-attachment;
seek it by directing all your energies upward.

227
Stimulating the *chakras*

The awakening of energy in the *chakras* of the spine
comes not merely by stimulation,
but by directing the energy upward, toward the brain.
Mere stimulation exposes one
to long-established habits of involvement in outwardness.
Such stimulation tends to induce
a sense of excitement, even of nervousness.
This sensation, emanating from the *chakras* themselves,
flows outward from the inner Self to the world,
enmeshing one in it further.
Instead, *relax* any energy you feel in the *chakras*:
channel it upward, and direct it
toward the center between the eyebrows:
the point of inner contact with God.

228

All is connected

Visualize a vast web—like that of a spider,
but with no lethal connotations.
See yourself poised on this web
as a single, glistening dewdrop.
Many other drops are on the same web,
all of them connected by the filaments of past associations,
each association woven by the great "Spider"
of Infinite Consciousness.
In this way, behold your oneness with all life.

229

Negation vs. affirmation

The nihilist — like many who try
to puzzle out the truth by the intellect alone —
feels no call to action;
he mocks at commitment of any kind,
and is more interested in clever theories than in truth.
In this respect he is sterile, like a hybrid seed.
And because he cannot, in himself, engender new life,
he robs others of whatever warmth of life they possess.
True, life-pulsating human beings,
and great teachers of wisdom like Jesus, Krishna,
and many others, issue a plea, instead,
to personal commitment,
and to the rewards of eternal bliss and love in God.

230

Seek heavenly, not earthly happiness

Sense pleasures resemble the satisfaction one feels
in scratching a mosquito bite:
the scratching feels good, but at the same time it hurts!
Seek deeper, longer-lasting satisfactions in life!
True happiness lies beneath the surface of sense awareness;
it lies in your soul, and in the fresh breeze
of inner soul-happiness.

231

Develop patience

Calming the mind is like watching the particles of dirt
in a glass of water
sink gradually to the bottom.
One cannot command the particles to settle.
If one lets the glass sit for a while, however,
those impurities will settle slowly on their own.
Those which rise to the surface, instead,
can be skimmed off.
In any case, develop a waiting, watchful attitude,
and everything in your life will turn out well.

232

The ego as a whirlpool

The ego lies at the center
of a self-created vortex.
Around it, all egoic desires revolve.

233

I, my, me, mine—and then: poor ME!

A person with an unhealthy ego is wholly focused
on his problems, worries, and complexes.
He broods on how others treat him,
and never thinks how he might help them.
He is a psychological whirlpool,
into which every interest is drawn—
to be drowned in ever-lower energy
and ever-diminishing enthusiasm for life.
His contractiveness is unhealthy, for it consumes his vitality,
distorts his perceptions of reality,
robs him of his natural ability to enjoy anything,
and, finally, imprisons him
in a dungeon of ever-dimming awareness
from which there will be, in this life, no escape.

234

Reason is a way station

The intellect can take us only partway
on our long evolutionary climb.
By clear reasoning, we may come to see
the limits of reason itself;
from that point, however, we must accept
that only the heart's endorsement
can provide the full certainty of true faith.

235

God, in Creation, is very shy!

God hides Himself in Creation.
He is like the banked embers of a smoldering fire.
Concealed by ashes, there may be a dim glow, here and there,
but the fire will burn openly only rarely.
When it does so burn, the display occurs only
in the lives of saints.

236

Lovemaking for partners

In physical union, seek always and above all to express love.
Love languishes, however, without respect,
and in respect one always feels a little distance.
True, loving union will occur, therefore, only occasionally.
Let your "lovemaking" be an occasion
to be approached even with a degree of awe and holy reverence.
In this way, human love can help you on your path to God.
Always remember, however, that sex also depletes one's energy.
Seek true union above all, therefore,
by embracing each other with heartfelt love;
then let your energy flow upward from there,
toward the spiritual eye.

237
Small-minded debate

Some people stubbornly pursue their own line of reasoning
as though no other could possibly exist.
They defend their convictions by the "Ostrich Method."
Have the courage to heed other lines of reasoning—
even accept them, if they are right.
Be willing, if necessary, to "turn on a dime."
After all, whatever is, simply *is*!

238

Wind of AUM

When no wind blows over the ocean,
its waters become relatively still.
Such was the Cosmic Spirit, before it manifested Creation.
When God created, the little ripples of causal manifestation
began their cosmic dance.
The waves then rose higher,
and the universe of light and energy emerged
from shadow to shimmering substance.
At last, God, satisfied so far,
began to dance with joy.
Also, however, in each individual wave
He permitted the thought of pride—and lo!
The physical universe heaved into manifestation.
Competition and brute force became almost necessary
to material accomplishment.
Matter took precedence over more subtle realities.
The storm of *Maya* began to rage,
and beings sought protection
in holes, caves, and other self-enclosing shelters.
Then began the fight for survival—
and, at last, the struggle for transcendence and return.

239

Grace

Grace can only be *received*, by tuning in to it.
It comes to us not so much by God's will as by our own.
We must offer ourselves to Him.
He will always be there, waiting for us.

240

Not only roses await you on the path!

The spiritual path is a minefield
strewn with "karmic bombs":
explosions of restlessness, eruptions of desire.
Make sure your heart's aspiration and determination
are always focused on God's angelic forces beyond,
cheering and waving you on to victory.

241

No cause for pride

Clouds in the sunset assume radiant, beautiful hues.
After the sunset, however,
those same clouds turn gray, then perhaps dark and ugly.
The sun it is which gives everything its beauty.
Look to yourself:
No glory will be possible unless it comes from God.

242
Inflicting hurt

Every time you hurt another living being,
you hurt yourself.
If you kick a wall, what is it that feels the most pain?
Your own foot, surely!

243
Inspire others

The way to help people out of ignorance
is to inspire in them a yearning for understanding.
Scolding them instead would be like
berating a blind man for his inability to see.

244
Love be your polestar

Let your love for others be like the needle of a compass,
which, no matter how often it is deflected,
turns back to its natural position, pointing north.
Even if others cease to love you,
remain always, even if only silently, their friend.

245
Be like a tree in flower

When someone speaks to you unkindly,
be like a flowering tree which, though stricken to its roots,
responds only by showering blossoms on its destroyer.
No matter how people treat you,
strew them with blossoms of kindness and sincerity.

246
A loyal friend always

Be like a bright star, shining steadily
through the dark night,
providing guidance, hope, and encouragement
to all who stumble and fall on life's darkened streets.
Shine with steadfast loyalty upon everyone,
whether friend or bitterest, if self-styled, enemy.
For all are your own, equally, in God.

247
Concentrate on good things

Concentrate, like a hummingbird,
on the brightly colored flowers of positive experience.
Sip only sweetness,
wherever your flight takes you.

248

Offer to all a free partnership in your life

Possessiveness, like a creeper,
squeezes the life out of any living being to which it clings.
Allow others free access to the air and sunlight,
and bless them with the independence to be themselves.

249

Changing habits

To try to change a habit without changing the mental state
on which it depends would be like trying
to stabilize a wobbly table:
Pressing down on one corner only raises its opposite.
Work first, therefore, at changing the attitudes
on which bad habits depend.

250
Mountaineering

Dogmas are like pitons, used by mountaineers
in their work.
The piton helps a climber to reach ever-higher levels;
once the pinnacle is reached, however,
the piton will serve him no more.
A great saint once said,
"It is helpful to be born into a religion,
but a misfortune to die in one!"

251
Towards inner freedom

Be like a fish in the sea of consciousness,
swimming freely everywhere.
Avoid the fishermen of delusion
who cast nets of bondage to catch unmindful fish.
Flow joyously, rather, on the sweeping tides of grace.

252

On going to the saints

When going to saints or to others who love God,
offer to them, above all, your love.
Seek from them especially that which will
free you from ego-bondage.
To seek less from them would be like digging
for mushrooms in a gold mine.

253

Applause?

Depend not on applause.
Adulation, to a famous person,
can be like many admiring hands
on a delicate vase.
Their caresses may inadvertently crush.

254
Enjoying the divine banquet

The experience of God is forever varied—exquisitely so.
It can come even in the form of
a thousand delicious tastes all crushed into one.
Look to Him with the confidence of a child in its mother.
Then you will find yourself marveling to think,
"Why, for so long, did I turn away?"!

255
God wants you more than you could possibly want Him!

God's love, once felt in the heart,
is so attractive that it steals away from the world
all our love for it.
His love overwhelms every lesser desire.
The Hindu Scriptures describe Him as *rasa*:
Supremely Relishable.
St. Jean Vianney once said,
"If you only knew how much God loves you,
you would die for joy!"

About the Author

A prolific author, accomplished composer, playwright, and artist, and a world-renowned spiritual teacher, Swami Kriyananda (1926–2013) referred to himself simply as a close disciple of the great God-realized master, Paramhansa Yogananda. He met his guru at the age of twenty-two, and served him during the last four years of the Master's life. He dedicated the rest of his life to sharing Yogananda's teachings throughout the world.

Kriyananda was born in Romania of American parents, and educated in Europe, England, and the United States. Philosophically and artistically inclined from youth, he soon came to question life's meaning and society's values. During a period of intense inward reflection, he discovered Yogananda's *Autobiography of a Yogi*, and immediately traveled three thousand miles from New York to California to meet the Master, who accepted him as a monastic disciple. Yogananda appointed him as the head of the monastery, authorized him to teach and give Kriya initiation in his name, and entrusted him with the missions of writing, teaching, and creating what he called "world brotherhood colonies."

Kriyananda founded the first such community, Ananda Village, in the Sierra Nevada foothills of Northern California in 1968. Ananda is recognized as one of the most successful intentional communities in the world today. It has served as a model for other such communities that he founded subsequently in the United States, Europe, and India

Further Explorations

CRYSTAL CLARITY PUBLISHERS

If you enjoyed this title, Crystal Clarity Publishers invites you to deepen your spiritual life through many additional resources based on the teachings of Paramhansa Yogananda. We offer books, e-books, audiobooks, yoga and meditation videos, and a wide variety of inspirational and relaxation music composed by Swami Kriyananda.

See a listing of books below, visit our secure website for a complete online catalog, or place an order for our products.

crystalclarity.com
800.424.1055 | clarity@crystalclarity.com
14618 Tyler Foote Rd. | Nevada City, CA 95959

ANANDA WORLDWIDE

Crystal Clarity Publishers is the publishing house of Ananda, a worldwide spiritual movement founded by Swami Kriyananda, a direct disciple of Paramhansa Yogananda. Ananda offers resources and support for your spiritual journey through meditation instruction, webinars, online virtual community, email, and chat.

Ananda has more than 150 centers and meditation groups in over 45 countries, offering group guided meditations, classes and teacher training in meditation and yoga, and many other resources.

In addition, Ananda has developed eight residential communities in the US, Europe, and India. Spiritual communities are places where people live together in a spirit of cooperation and friendship, dedicated to a common goal. Spirituality is practiced in all areas of daily life: at school, at work, or in the home. Many Ananda communities offer internships during which one can stay and experience spiritual community firsthand.

For more information about Ananda communities or meditation groups near you, please visit ananda.org or call 530.478.7560.

THE EXPANDING LIGHT RETREAT

The Expanding Light is the largest retreat center in the world to share exclusively the teachings of Paramhansa Yogananda. Situated in the Ananda Village community near Nevada City, California, the center offers the opportunity to experience spiritual life in a contemporary ashram setting. The varied, year-round schedule of classes and programs on yoga, meditation, and spiritual practice includes Karma Yoga, personal retreat, spiritual travel, and online learning. Large groups are welcome.

The Ananda School of Yoga & Meditation offers certified yoga, yoga therapist, spiritual counselor, and meditation teacher trainings.

The teaching staff has years of experience practicing Kriya Yoga meditation and all aspects of Paramhansa Yogananda's teachings. You may come for a relaxed personal renewal, participating in ongoing activities as much or as little as you wish. The serene mountain setting, supportive staff, and delicious vegetarian meals provide an ideal environment for a truly meaningful stay, be it a brief respite or an extended spiritual vacation.

For more information, please visit expandinglight.org or call 800.346.5350.

ANANDA MEDITATION RETREAT

Set amidst seventy-two acres of beautiful meditation gardens and wild forest in Northern California's Sierra foothills, the Ananda Meditation Retreat is an ideal setting for a rejuvenating, inner experience.

The Meditation Retreat has been a place of deep meditation and sincere devotion for over fifty years. Long before that, the Native American Maidu tribe held this to be sacred land. The beauty and presence of the Divine are tangibly felt by all who visit here.

Studies show that being in nature and using techniques such as forest bathing can significantly reduce stress and blood pressure while strengthening your immune system, concentration, and level of happiness. The Meditation Retreat is the perfect place for quiet immersion in nature.

Plan a personal retreat, enjoy one of the guided retreats, or choose from a variety of programs led by the caring and joyful staff.

For more information or to make your reservation, please visit meditationretreat.org, email meditationretreat@ananda.org, or call 530.478.7557.

THE ORIGINAL 1946 UNEDITED EDITION OF
YOGANANDA'S SPIRITUAL MASTERPIECE

AUTOBIOGRAPHY OF A YOGI
Paramhansa Yogananda

Autobiography of a Yogi is one of the world's most acclaimed spiritual classics, with millions of copies sold. Named one of the Best 100 Spiritual Books of the twentieth century, this book helped launch and continues to inspire a spiritual awakening throughout the Western world.

Yogananda was the first yoga master of India whose mission brought him to settle and teach in the West. His firsthand account of his life experiences in India includes childhood revelations, stories of his visits to saints and masters, and long-secret teachings of yoga and Self-realization that he first made available to the Western reader.

This reprint of the original 1946 edition is free from textual changes made after Yogananda's passing in 1952. This updated edition includes bonus materials: the last chapter that Yogananda wrote in 1951, also without posthumous changes, the eulogy Yogananda wrote for Gandhi, and a new foreword and afterword by Swami Kriyananda, one of Yogananda's close, direct disciples.

Also available in Spanish and Hindi from Crystal Clarity Publishers.

PARAMHANSA YOGANANDA
A Biography with Personal Reflections and Reminiscences
Swami Kriyananda

Paramhansa Yogananda's life was filled with astonishing accomplishments. And yet in his classic autobiography, he wrote more about the saints he'd met than about his own spiritual attainments. Yogananda's direct disciple, Swami Kriyananda, relates the untold story of this great master and world teacher: his teenage miracles, his challenges in coming to America, his national lecture campaigns, his struggles to fulfill his world-changing mission amid incomprehension and painful betrayals, and his ultimate triumphant achievement.

Kriyananda's subtle grasp of his guru's inner nature and outward mission reveals Yogananda's many-sided greatness. Includes many never-before-published anecdotes and an insider's view of the Master's last years.

WHISPERS FROM ETERNITY
A Book of Answered Prayers
Paramhansa Yogananda
Edited by his disciple, Swami Kriyananda

Many poetic works can inspire, but few have the power to change lives. These poems and prayers have been "spiritualized" by Paramhansa Yogananda: Each has drawn a response from the Divine. Yogananda was not only a master poet, whose imagery here is as vivid and alive as when first published in 1949: He was a spiritual master, an avatar.

He encouraged his disciples to read from *Whispers from Eternity* every day, explaining that through these verses he could guide them after his passing. But this book is not for his disciples alone. It is for spiritual aspirants of any tradition who wish to drink from this fountain of pure inspiration and wisdom.

THE NEW PATH
My Life with Paramhansa Yogananda
Swami Kriyananda

Winner of the 2010 Eric Hoffer Award for Best Self-Help/Spiritual Book
Winner of the 2010 USA Book News Award for Best Spiritual Book

The New Path is a moving revelation of one man's search for lasting happiness. After rejecting the false promises offered by modern society, J. Donald Walters found himself (much to his surprise) at the feet of Paramhansa Yogananda, asking to become his disciple. How he got there, trained with the Master, and became Swami Kriyananda makes fascinating reading.

The rest of the book is the fullest account by far of what it was like to live with and be a disciple of that great man of God.

Anyone hungering to learn more about Yogananda will delight in the hundreds of stories of life with a great avatar and the profound lessons they offer. This book is an ideal complement to *Autobiography of a Yogi*.

GOD AS DIVINE MOTHER
Wisdom and Inspiration for Love and Acceptance
Paramhansa Yogananda and Swami Kriyananda

We long for a God who loves us exactly as we are, who doesn't judge us but rather helps and encourages us in achieving our highest potential. In this book, discover the teachings and inspirations on Divine Mother from Paramhansa Yogananda. These teachings are universal: No matter your religious background, or lack thereof, you will find these messages of love and acceptance resonating on a soul-level.

"The role of the Divine Mother is to draw all Her children, all self-aware beings everywhere, back to oneness with God."

In this book, you will discover: Who is Divine Mother?; How to develop the heart's natural love; What attitudes draw Her grace; How to tune in to Divine Mother. Included also are over thirty poems and prayers dedicated to God in the form of Divine Mother, as well as original chants and songs by the authors.

INTUITION FOR STARTERS
Swami Kriyananda

Every day in our hectic world we are tasked with multiple decisions based on either not enough information or too much information. Problem solving when clear-cut answers are elusive is stressful.

Is there a way to know how to make the best choice? Yes! through developing our faculty of intuition.

Often thought of as something vague and undefinable, intuition is the ability to perceive truth directly not by reason, logic, or analysis, but by simply knowing from within.

This book explains how within each of us lies the ability to perceive the answers we need, and shows how to access the powerful stream of creative energy which lies beneath the surface of our conscious mind: the superconscious.

Step-by-step exercises, advice, and guidance reveal the once mysterious faculty of intuition to be an ally and an accessible fountain of wisdom to be found within each of us.

ONCE AND FUTURE CHRIST
Where East Meets West
Nayaswami Hriman McGilloway

There is a great need in these times for a deeper and more universal understanding of the teachings of Jesus Christ.

Paramhansa Yogananda came to America in 1920 to focus the light of India's timeless and timely wisdom upon the teachings of Jesus Christ. In *Once and Future Christ*, Nayaswami Hriman McGilloway expands upon that message with the inclusion of modern scientific discoveries and an exploration of the similarities and relationships between Christianity and Yoga.

This book describes the inevitable evolution of Christian dogma towards greater inclusivity. The pathway of this future evolution leads to an understanding that the individual soul's relationship to God is the goal of the spiritual life.

THE WISDOM OF YOGANANDA *series*

The Wisdom of Yogananda series features writings of Paramhansa Yogananda not available elsewhere. These books capture the Master's expansive and compassionate wisdom, his sense of fun, and his practical spiritual guidance. The books include writings from his earliest years in America, in an approachable, easy-to-read format. The words of the Master are presented with minimal editing, to capture the fresh and original voice of one of the most highly regarded spiritual teachers of the twentieth century.

The series titles include:

How to Be Happy All the Time
Karma and Reincarnation
How to Love and Be Loved
How to Be a Success
How to Have Courage, Calmness, and Confidence
How to Achieve Glowing Health and Vitality

How to Awaken Your True Potential
The Man Who Refused Heaven
How to Face Life's Changes
How to Spiritualize Your Life
How to Live Without Fear
How to Increase Your Magnetism

For more titles in books, audiobooks, spoken word,
music, and videos, and for a complete online catalog
of Crystal Clarity Publishers products, visit **crystalclarity.com**.